Manatees

Manatees

Mary Ann McDonald

THE CHILD'S WORLD®, INC.

Library of Congress Cataloging-in-Publication Data
McDonald, Mary Ann.
Manatees / by Mary Ann McDonald.
p. cm.
Includes index.
Summary: Describes the physical characteristics, behavior, and habitat
of manatees, as well as the danger of extinction they face.
ISBN 1-56766-475-X 1.
1. Manatees—Juvenile literature.
[1. Manatees. 2. Endangered species.] I. Title.
QL737.S63M368 1998
599.55—dc21 97-38097
CIP
AC

Photo Credits

© Brandon D. Cole: 2, 26
© Daniel J. Cox/Natural Exposures: 10, 23
© Marilyn Kazmers/Sharksong: 6, 20, 24
© Mark J. Thomas/Dembinsky Photo Assoc. Inc.: 9, 16
© Schafer-Hill/Tony Stone Images: cover
© Stephen Frink/Tony Stone Images: 15
© Stuart Westmorland/Tony Stone Images: 19
© Tom Campbell's Photographic: 13, 29, 30

On the cover...

Front cover: This manatee is swimming just under the surface of the water.
Page 2: This manatee is floating in clear waters.

Table of Contents

Long ago, explorers sailed around the world. As they traveled, they saw many exciting and beautiful things. Sometimes the sailors would see things they did not understand. When this happened, they would make up stories. Some sailors thought they saw people that had tails like fishes. They called them *mermaids*.

But the explorers did not look closely at these strange creatures. They saw them only from far away. Today, we know what the sailors were looking at—manatees!

What Are Manatees?

Manatees belong to a group of animals called **mammals**. Mammals have warm bodies and feed their babies milk from their bodies. Most mammals also have hair on their bodies, but manatees do not. Cows, dogs, and people are mammals, too.

Manatees sometimes float near the surface of the water. When they do, their heads and front arms, or **flippers**, stay above the water. The flippers are shaped like short paddles. The manatees' tails stretch out and float, too. From far away, a floating manatee looks a lot like a floating person. That is what the sailors of long ago saw.

These manatees are swimming and playing. ⇒

Manatees live in both freshwater and saltwater. That means they can live in rivers and lakes, and also in the salty ocean. Manatees like warm water. That is why they are found mostly in the warm areas of the world. Africa and South America are two countries that have manatees. The United States has manatees, too. A few manatees still live in Florida's warm rivers.

What Do Manatees Look Like?

Manatees look a little like seals. They have rounded bodies with flat, paddle-shaped tails. They are often gray or brown, and they have large, round faces with stiff whiskers. At the end of each flipper, manatees have fingernails just as you do. Manatees can grow up to 13 feet long and weigh almost 1,500 pounds.

This manatee is breathing air from the surface. ⇒

Manatees can die if the water they are swimming in is too cold. That is why they have a thin layer of fat under their skin. This fat is called **blubber**. It helps to keep the manatees warm. Manatees are not the only sea animals that have blubber. Whales and seals also depend on blubber to keep them warm.

It is easy to see the blubber around this manatee's neck. ⇒

Manatees eat only plants. In fact, they are sometimes called *sea cows* because they eat many different kinds of plants, just as farm cows do. Manatees use their strong lips to tear plants from the muddy bottom. They also use their flippers to scoop up floating plants.

⇐ This manatee is eating a floating water plant.

Manatees have flat, wide teeth to grind their food. As these teeth wear down, they move to the front of the manatee's mouth and fall out. New teeth are always replacing the worn-out ones.

Manatees eat a lot of food. Some can eat almost 150 pounds in one day! But they are not very active animals. In fact, after they finish eating, they like to take naps. Most of a manatee's day is spent either resting or eating.

This manatee is resting on a river bottom. ⇒

Manatees often talk to each other by touching. They greet other manatees by pressing their noses together, which looks like kissing. They also touch with their flippers and tails. Touching makes the manatees feel happy and safe.

Manatees also use sounds to talk to each other. Babies often squeal or squeak to talk to their mothers. Other manatees make sounds when they are frightened or angry. And some manatees make sounds just to let others know where they are.

⇐ Manatees like these two like to kiss and touch.

What Are Baby Manatees Like?

Baby manatees are called **calves**. They look just like adult manatees, only smaller. Even so, they are very big to you and me—baby manatees are four feet long and weigh 70 pounds!

A mother and her calf stay together for two years. During this time, the mother teaches her baby what foods to eat and where to find them. She also teaches her calf how to escape danger. When the calf is ready, it leaves its mother to live on its own.

This calf is following its mother while she swims. ⇒

Do Manatees Have Any Enemies?

The manatee's only enemy is people. Some people kill manatees for their meat or bones. But most manatees are killed or hurt by boats. The sharp blades of the motors can cut slow-moving manatees as they swim and eat. Bigger boats sometimes crush manatees resting in shallow waters. And some manatees drown after getting tangled in fishing nets.

⇐ This manatee's tail was badly damaged by a boat motor.

Are Manatees in Danger?

Manatees are **endangered** animals. That means there are very few manatees left in the wild. Too many are dying because people are careless in the water. We drive fast boats and throw garbage into places where manatees live. We also destroy the plants the manatees need to eat. To save the manatees, we must learn to be more careful.

⇐ Manatees like to swim in quiet waters.

Many governments now protect wild manatees. Areas where they live have been turned into parks with very firm rules. In these areas, boats and swimmers are not allowed. This keeps the waters clean and free of dangerous motor blades. It also keeps the water quiet and calm so the manatees are happy.

This sign tells people to slow down because manatees are nearby. ⇒

Where Can You Go to See Manatees?

Some parks have viewing areas where people can watch the manatees. If you ever go to a manatee park, stop by one of these areas. Watch how the beautiful manatees float, eat, and play. Then you will understand how important it is to protect them. If we all work together, these wonderful animals will be around for many years to come.

⇐ This manatee is swimming near a viewing area.

Glossary

blubber (BLUH–ber)
Blubber is a layer of fat underneath the skin that helps sea mammals keep warm. Manatees have a very thin layer of blubber.

calves (KAVZ)
Calves are baby manatees. Calves drink milk from their mothers.

endangered (en–DANE–jerd)
When a type of animal is endangered, it is in danger of dying out. Manatees are said to be endangered because there are few left in the wild.

flippers (FLIH–perz)
Flippers are a manatee's arms. Manatees use their paddle-shaped flippers for swimming and eating.

mammals (MA–mullz)
Mammals are animals that have warm bodies and feed their babies milk from their bodies. Manatees, cows, dogs, and people are all mammals.

Index